The Threefold Cord

A Play

Scott Marshall

Samuel French — London
www.samuelfrench-london.co.uk

Copyright © 2010 by Scott Marshall
All Rights Reserved

THE THREEFOLD CORD is fully protected under the copyright laws of the British Commonwealth, including Canada, the United States of America, and all other countries of the Copyright Union. All rights, including professional and amateur stage productions, recitation, lecturing, public reading, motion picture, radio broadcasting, television and the rights of translation into foreign languages are strictly reserved.

ISBN 978-0-573-11436-6

www.samuelfrench.co.uk

www.samuelfrench.com

FOR AMATEUR PRODUCTION ENQUIRIES

UNITED KINGDOM AND WORLD EXCLUDING NORTH AMERICA

plays@samuelfrench.co.uk

020 7255 4302/01

Each title is subject to availability from Samuel French, depending upon country of performance.

CAUTION: Professional and amateur producers are hereby warned that *THE THREEFOLD CORD* is subject to a licensing fee. Publication of this play does not imply availability for performance. Both amateurs and professionals considering a production are strongly advised to apply to the appropriate agent before starting rehearsals, advertising, or booking a theatre. A licensing fee must be paid whether the title is presented for charity or gain and whether or not admission is charged.

The Professional Rights in this play are controlled by Samuel French Ltd, 24-32 Stephenson Way, London NW1 2HD.

No one shall make any changes in this title for the purpose of production. No part of this book may be reproduced, stored in a retrieval system, or transmitted in any form, by any means, now known or yet to be invented, including mechanical, electronic, photocopying, recording, videotaping, or otherwise, without the prior written permission of the publisher. No one shall upload this title, or part of this title, to any social media websites.

The right of Scott Marshall to be identified as author of this work has been asserted in accordance with Section 77 of the Copyright, Designs and Patents Act 1988.

CHARACTERS

Victoria Selgrove, celebrated actress wife of a barrister, expensively, tastefully dressed, likeable, though very self-centred, 40s
Millicent, intelligent, well-educated, rather retiring, much less outgoing than Victoria. Also likeable, 40s
Dexie, lively, feisty prostitute. Kind, vocal, likeable, early 20s
Sir Marcus Pennington, successful barrister, husband of Victoria. Magnetic, energetic personality.

All characters age by 20–25 years from act one to act two. The three ladies, in particular, must show this time passage

AUTHOR'S NOTE

The tripartite staging needs to reflect (and it may be done very simply with 2 or 3 basic props) the three homes or bases of the three women who remain on stage throughout the play. As each spends most time addressing the audience, suitable props would be useful, such as a screen, chair, small table or ornament for each actress. Lighting should be able to cross-fade from one character, in her location, to another. An elaborately dressed, composite setting is quite unnecessary, though certainly possible. The three women may have frequent (if slight) changes of costume, suggesting the passage of time or in keeping with the lines they are speaking.

Scott Marshall

And if one prevail against him, two shall withstand him; and a threefold cord is not quickly broken.

Ecclesiastes 4 v.12

For Olivia

ACT I

Victoria When the girls were young they used to ask me, Beatrice in particular, questions about him like "Does Daddy love you?" or "How do you know Daddy loves you?" They rarely saw us together, you see. Away at boarding school all term, on trips here and there during the holidays — skiing, French exchange.

Pause

When they were at home Marcus was so seldom here, either staying in the club or involved in lengthy sittings. And of course I was rehearsing, playing in London or on tour. It was so difficult for us all to be together at one time. Not that it worried any of us greatly — Beatrice a little perhaps, she always tended to be a little clingy — but Marcus was so busy, the girls had their own friends and so many parties — what a non-stop social whirl these young people have nowadays — and of course I had not only my stage work but quite a bit of television and radio work as well.

Pause

Nigel Lymington actually changed some of the sequences last year for *Women in Chains*. Swapped some of them right round just to accommodate me. One of my very favourite people. Such a talented director — gives, gives, gives all the time. His *Cherry Orchard* must be in line for a BAFTA this year. Wonderful production, so totally agrarian. He wanted me for Ranevsky but I was too tied down with *The Importance* and the RSC wouldn't release me. I could have wept. Don't misunderstand me, Rona Magnus gave a very acceptable performance, but it was only that, a performance. I mean, really, the soul, the Russian heart was missing, don't you think? No depth, no internal dimension which Nigel claims I always bring to my roles. But, of course, don't misunderstand me, Rona is frightfully good. In certain parts.

Pause

Anyway, as I was saying, it was never easy for the four of us to get together. But all families have problems, don't they? From *Coronation Street* to the Windsors. We are all soap operas really.

Lights cross-fade from Victoria to Millicent

Millicent Actually, Sir Marcus was one of Clifford's best friends, soul mates at Harrow, Peterhouse and in chambers together, best man at our wedding as Clifford was at his. So, inevitably I got to know him quite well.

Pause

I knew of his reputation, of course, from Clifford. "A right randy old lecher" he called him once so, naturally, forewarned was forearmed, when he occasionally came up to stay, and he did seem to enjoy Chalfont St Clements.

Pause

When Marcus did visit us he rarely brought Victoria with him. She was always playing in the West End or rehearsing somewhere like Chichester or Bristol, touring before coming to London. Very talented, it goes without saying, and she matured over the years so slowly. Admirable timing, really. No rush at all. Ever so clever.

Pause

It was funny you know — when Clifford would call Marcus, "A very devil for the wenches", or recount a tale of old Mar's latest conquest, I could hear more than a slight note of envy in my husband's voice.

Pause

I remember saying once to Clifford, "It's a jolly good job Victoria knows nothing of his philandering or we would have a really dramatic performance to behold" and he roared with laughter, "Of course she knows all about him. She may be a dumb blonde, at times, but the talented Victoria is no fool. She has introduced him to at least half his harem in the past and when old Mar is off on his latest pursuit, she does quite a bit of entertaining of her own. Oh yes, what's sauce for the gander and all that. The Nelsonian blind eye is an unspoken arrangement they both seem more than happy with. Don't

Act I

underestimate Vicks, star of stage and screen. Tough as old boots and more than a match for old Mar."

Pause

So, two promiscuous animals in the one family. My husband does keep such unusual company, but interesting, one must admit.

Lights cross-fade from Millicent to Dexie

Dexie Our first meeting? Of course I remember it. How could I forget? I must have been about twenty-four or twenty-five and I was on Ridley Street, between the bridge and the old station. Getting dark it was and he come round the corner, out of Jervis Lane, like a train, taking a short cut, head down and he barged straight into me. His briefcase went in one direction and I went in the other. Typical-like, he went after the briefcase which had flew open and papers, they was everywhere. Scrabbling around trying to pick them all up and shouting at me, over his shoulder, to help him. I could have been bleeding unconscious for all he noticed.

Pause

We got the pages and files all back in the briefcase and then what does he do? Proceeds to give me what's what for bumping into him! No apology or nothing, just real annoyed he was. Not half as annoyed as me though and I let him have it — both of us sitting there, on the floor, in Ridley Street. I don't remember all the names I called him, but my uncle Bert would have known most of them for I picked them up from him. "Where did you learn language like that?" he says with a sort of surprised look on his face. "Where did you learn manners like that?" I replies, "I could sue you, I could, for damages. I think my arm's broke" and that was the first thing calmed him down. Course it wasn't broke, it wasn't even hurt but he needed something saying to him to make him think of me and not himself. "Show me", he says and he took my arm and I squealed as if it was about to fall off.

Pause

Then, what does he do next? He brings out his wallet, takes a twenty pound note out and tries to stick it in my hand. He'd nice hands, long fingers, not rough at all. I felt that straight away. Always noticed a punter's hands in those days, I did. Anyway I says, "What do you think you're doing, mister?" and push his hand away. I could see he was surprised at that and I could see he was staring at me a lot. Not just ordinary looking — but staring sort of interested-like. To be honest, I would have took the twenty quid and that would have been it but for two things. One, that look he was giving me — he was definitely interested and two, that wallet was stuffed with notes. I remember, at that second, thinking, here's a challenge, Dexie, what can you take him for?

Pause

So I tries to stand up and he does help me, I remember that, and I was holding the broken arm, trying to remember which one it is and I produce a few tears at the same time. That's always chancy, cos it can act in two different ways — put them right off, steer clear-like, or get them sort of protective and arm round you. I judged him wrong for he was the first type, steps back and looks as if he's going to bolt for it. So I switches off the waterworks and quite formal-like asks if he would be gentleman enough to help me home, cos my place was just round the corner over the shops and I felt a bit unsteady. "Don't touch me" I says to him, sort of re-assuring him that he was safe enough, "But I feel as if I might faint before I make home". He looks at his watch and I could see he didn't know what to do, so I do a slight stagger, nothing too dramatic-like, no big deal, but just a little fall back against the wall, clutching the broken arm and that does it. He takes another look at his watch, mutters something about not going to make the train now, and I knew I had him. I also knew I was going to make that wallet lighter for him. I never mistake that look, you see, when they're interested. Know what I mean?

Lights cross-fade from Dexie to Victoria

Victoria School functions were often the best opportunities for our getting together — the four of us, I mean, as a family, but even that could prove difficult at times. One November for example, Marcus and I arranged to go down to Montcliffe to see the school play. Beatrice was so excited because Claudia had another part. Claudia — not her! I'm afraid there's a lot of young sister hero-worship for big sister with my two girls. Claudia can do no wrong as far as Beatrice is concerned and Claudia does play on it shamefully. Would you believe it, at home, during the holidays, I have seen Bea taking up Claudia's breakfast to her in bed.

Act I

Pause

Well, that's not quite right. I didn't actually see Bea doing it — or I would have put my foot down — but Sandy, Mrs Sanders, who comes in to tidy up and do the ironing and cooking and so on, was in the kitchen preparing my lightly scrambled egg — that's the only possible way I can eat an egg — fried or poached eggs look so insolent on a plate I always feel — and she said Bea was in and out with Claudia's tray in a flash. Singing away — blissfully happy! A strange child, Beatrice, and so conscious of her teeth, but what can one do. Claudia has such perfect features. We're all agreed Bea takes after Marcus's side of the family.

Pause

Anyway, the school play! They were to do *The Boy Friend*, such fun and, according to Bea, nobody could dance the Charleston as divinely as Claudia. Bea managed to get involved as one of the ten man stage crew and in every phone call she raved, simply raved, about Claudia's dancing. "She looks so like you, Ma, in some of your old photos", she would say. A little exaggeration, I'm sure, but she was so excited. Then the bombshell!

Pause

Mrs McAndrew, the physics teacher, who was directing the show, suddenly left at half-term, to take up an appointment in a boys' comprehensive school in Doncaster. Doncaster! What a physics teacher would know about the dramatic arts, I hesitate to think, although I believe she also taught some home economics and divinity. So off she went leaving little Miss Perdy to take over. Now, Miss Perdy is a most intense little lady, enthusiastic certainly, but one would have to say vague in the extreme. She cannot be much more than four feet in height with very short cropped hair. Not unlike the cut I had when playing *St Joan* at the Haymarket with Barry Jordan as the Inquisitor. Yes, Barry Jordan! I know, amazing! Whatever, *The Times* or was it the *Telegraph*, one or the other, said it was the most stunning Shaw of its generation. "O God that madest this beautiful earth, when will it be ready to receive Thy Saints?" Lovely, lovely part — I brought tears to my own eyes every performance.

Pause

However, I was speaking of little Miss Perdy. Oh yes, distinctly odd, quite distrait at times. I had spoken to her on one or two occasions at Montcliffe, parents' weekends mostly, and never understood a word she was saying. Well, apparently she was assisting Mrs McAndrew with the production when that good lady suddenly shot north. The next thing the girls knew *The Boy Friend* had been called off.

Pause

Claudia didn't seem too upset. She's a very, very phlegmatic young lady. Never lets too much disturb her. A whole galaxy of As and A stars at GCSE, right across the board, absolutely clean sweep, and all she did was raise her eyebrows and say, "As one expected". Marcus said she must go up to Cambridge but she's talking of some pools-forecasting or science of probability course at Sunderland Polytechnic — very single-minded, her father's daughter! So, as expected, she was quite unmoved but dear Beatrice was distraught. She does take things so much to heart, poor thing!

Pause

Next, little Miss Perdy called the cast together, told them *The Boy Friend* was much too frivolous for her to direct, it didn't speak to her and therefore she couldn't communicate with it but a school play had to be produced and she was changing the choice to *The Caretaker*.

Pause

Now, I ask you, *The Caretaker*. A cast of three men to be produced in an all girls' school! Now don't get me wrong, I know the play very well — who doesn't — and Harold and Antonia are very dear friends. He writes some intriguing, enigmatic theatre and of course Antonia's biographies are wonderful too, but *The Caretaker* at Montcliffe, I don't think so.

Pause

Immediately Beatrice told me, I phoned Miss Cheshire the next morning to express my concerns. She was quite cool — polite of course — but quite unmoved by my concerns. She said she had every confidence in Miss Perdy's ability to direct a school performance in keeping with the dramatic reputation of Montcliffe. I was sorely tempted to ask,

Act I 7

"What dramatic reputation?" I mean, until Claudia began to play lead roles, the school play was simply an annual agony for parents to suffer in soporific silence. The Bishop always slept through it. However the Headmistress asked if I might have an opportunity sometime to drop in on a rehearsal and proffer some advice. I declined of course and I think by the end of our rather terse conversation she had realized that the whole thing might be a mistake. Not, of course, that she said so, in so many words, just looked forward to seeing Sir Marcus and myself at one of the performances. Because, who had been cast as the caretaker — the devious old homeless tramp? Why, Claudia of course.

Lights cross-fade from Victora to Millicent

Millicent My blissful days in Chalfont St Clements were to be short-lived. Three days before his forty-second birthday Clifford dropped dead. It was a great shock. We had been married just six years. The autopsy said a coronary thrombosis. The first time I had heard the phrase "coronary thrombosis". I always thought "coronary" had to do with a crown or a coronation but there we are. Fit and active one moment, slumped dead in a taxi outside the Old Bailey the next. So sudden, so…final. It's a frightful thing not to be able to say goodbye.

Pause

They said I was very brave throughout it all. In truth, I don't remember much about it. George and Hazel arrived from Scotland and they took over. George arranged the funeral service, the undertakers, the flowers — just ... everything. I was so grateful. There's nothing really prepares you for that type of organization. Funeral announcements, notices in the papers, choice of hymns — all that sort of thing. Marcus called, of course, on one or two occasions and Victoria was with him at one time. And I did hear George saying at least a few times what a great help Marcus was. I know he was upset. He and Clifford had been very close from school days, even though like chalk and cheese.

Pause

The day of the funeral passed so quickly. I was dreading it naturally, but it all went so swiftly. Action-packed wouldn't be inappropriate to describe it. Doctor Glenn had insisted upon my taking some tablets as soon as I got up that morning and frankly, I think that had a lot to do with my much admired stiff upper lip throughout the day. Such a blur, the family gathering in the morning, Hazel and Celia Swinney serving endless cups of coffee. Celia always comes up trumps in an emergency. The two brothers, George and David greeting people. I remember the black ties and so many keeping coats on. One elderly man, very bald with florid cheeks and a red scarf, sitting in Clifford's chair, coughing incessantly. Then he was drinking a glass of water someone had brought him. It was bitterly cold. I recall Victoria, at one stage, holding my hand in the kitchen and talking very quietly. I have no recollection of what she said. Marcus stood just behind her and I'm almost certain I saw tears in his eyes. Then he was gone and I was sitting with George and Hazel in the back seat of the funeral car.

Pause

The church, St Michael's of course, was so cold. Everyone had their coats on. Two things I remember quite clearly. Looking at the coffin and refusing to believe that Clifford, my Clifford, was lying dead inside it. I expected him at any minute to appear in the aisle and slip in beside me. And the other thing was the singing. Like a poor male voice choir. No soprano voices, all heavy, dirge-like bass voices. "The day thou gavest Lord is ended. The darkness falls at thy behest." I wanted to hear something uplifting, some joyful, joyous sounds of happiness and thanksgiving for Clifford's life. It was a good life and shouldn't end in such a solemn grim way. That's what I thought as the vicar spoke. I know he mentioned me once or twice for Hazel squeezed my arm each time, but I never heard his words. And the red-scarfed man, I heard him, still coughing. Poor man, maybe he was ill and shouldn't have been there. I remember asking someone, Marcus, I think, who he was but I can't remember the name.

Pause

George and Hazel wanted me to go back to Scotland with them and stay for a few weeks but I couldn't do that. I knew if I had done, I could never have returned to Chalfont. Too many memories walking into an empty home. Would I see my husband sitting in his chair or an elderly mourner coughing sorely into his red muffler?

Pause

I did go to Edinburgh for three or four days but despite George and

Act I

Hazel's assurances I knew I had to return home then. I had already stayed longer than I intended. Clifford used to say something about house guests being like fish, going off after three days. So I returned to Chalfont, almost certain that I would shortly be paying Clarke and Bamford a visit to see about putting our lovely home on the market. I didn't think I could live there without Clifford.

Pause

I returned home on a Monday. On Tuesday I had a phone call from an old friend. Could he call to see me? I told Marcus I would be at home on Friday, "Seven o'clock," he said, "We'll go out."

Lights cross-fade from Millicent to Dexie

Dexie Well, I was dead right, wasn't I? About that interested look. He stays the night with me, over the Quickspin Laundrette, a good name that really, for his performance, and when he leaves in the morning, before seven it was, I had one fifty quid in my bottom drawer. I never carry a lot of notes in my purse. Always leave them under my smalls in the bottom drawer. Safe as houses! No one's to have their hand on those, at least till I'm wearing them. Well... it's my job, ain't it!

Pause

Not a bad catch really, I thought, after he went rushing off the next morning. If I could make him a regular punter I'd be quids in. And he had lovely hands. I knew he wasn't a brickie or a grave digger with those mitts. I told him he should have nail gloss on with those fingers and he laughed at that. Wanted to borrow mine and then he tried to grab my foot to put it on my toes. He got a kick in the belly for his trouble, not too hard-like, but enough for me to see how soft he was for his age. Like, he was no spring chicken. In his early forties I would say he was.

Pause

He asked me what job I had and I could see he was serious. He didn't see I was on the game so I said what I always say, if I have to, that I work in a florist's. I know Angie in "Fragrance and Flowers" and if anyone ever checks up with her, she would always say I worked part time with her. Good sort, Angie! Her older sister used to work the square before some scumbag hit her over the head with a breezeblock one night. They was both high as kites but it's no excuse, is it? That's when I first met Angie, when we were both visiting her sister in Saint Mary's. She had two nippers as well, Sharon, not Angie, and I helped to look after them for a few days, picked them up from school and so on, until she came out of hospital, then she went to live in Southampton. She had some relatives there, an aunt and uncle, who was going to help her recover. Wouldn't fancy being hit with a lump of concrete, would you? You have to be so bloody careful nowadays. Anyway I don't do drugs, not now anyway, and I don't smoke. I'm a real little goodie two shoes, me. Me and Angie have kept in touch, though she's not a best mate or anything like that, I can't really say I have a best mate, not since I left Kilburn.

Pause

I asked him what he did and he was all hush-hush at first. Wouldn't say a dickey bird but I kept at him and I told him I knew from his posh voice that he was no bookie's runner. Eventually he told me but he made me promise, first, that I would tell no one. He wouldn't even tell me his name at first and when I heard it I could see why. Imagine having to tell anyone you're called Fitzwilliam Darcy. I could hardly keep my face straight when he told me. "Fitzwilliam," I said, "where the heck did that come from? William I could understand but how come the Fitz bit?" But he just laughed. He was quite a joker was Fitz, but I reckoned I had his number.

Lights cross-fade from Dexie to Victoria

Victoria As it turned out Marcus wasn't able to see *The Caretaker*, quelle surprise! The day before we were to travel something cropped up in court, a colleague took ill and there was nobody else capable of stepping in at such short notice so Marcus spent that evening pouring over some brief to appear in court the next morning. I'm not convinced that some postponement or deferment of some kind, couldn't have been arranged but Marcus was quite adamant. "Your daughter will be shattered if you miss her big performance", I said to him. "As I am," he replied, "but in this instance a millionaire city embezzler, probably going down from seven to ten, must take precedence over two hours of Pinter. Claudia will understand." He gave me a good luck card that he had written for her and I knew there would be a twenty pound note inside it. His conscience money.

Pause

Act I 11

I rang Julian Bandell and he jumped at the opportunity to accompany me to Montcliffe. "Virgin territory, Vicks", was his response, the naughty boy! The press were still drooling over his Romeo at the National. Such a talent and only a year out of RADA. I imagined the girls would be thrilled to see him too. The boarders led very protected lives during term-time as one can imagine. As Claudia so dryly put it last summer, "The only hormonal stimulation we have here in Alcatraz is the sight of old Charlie cutting the grass and he's ninety if he's a day".

Pause

Julian and I drove down to Montcliffe on Friday afternoon. It's such a long drive there was no point in rushing back so we made a weekend of it. He was such exhilarating company and so very fit! I must say the girls and staff made quite a fuss over us both. We spoke to the cast after curtain and they were so excited about that. Perhaps a shade more at Julian's presence than at mine. I was, after all, Claudia's mother rather than Victoria Selgrove. The play itself? Well, I think the less one says about that the better. Claudia held it all together, quite beautifully and her East End accent was simply stunning, but the production! Miss Perdy had decided against giving it the kitchen sink setting – gas stove, clothes horse, coal bucket and lawn mower etc. Oh no! She transposed it to a very chic, up-market Chelsea flat with music from Tosca and La Boheme belting out, almost non-stop and at such a volume! She is quite a Puccini freak apparently, the little poisoned dwarf director, but there's a time and place surely! And Pinter's *Caretaker* was not it! I heard her saying afterwards to some of the stunned parents that unlike Verdi or Wagner, Puccini speaks to her. I just wonder what he says. I would imagine, something like "Not so bloody loud."

Lights cross-fade from Victoria to Millicent

Millicent Looking back, I'm still not clear why I ever agreed to his calling. I mean, there was absolutely no reason why he shouldn't but it had always been to see Clifford before. At least I assu… Well, anyway, he was Clifford's dearest friend and I felt Clifford would have been hurt had I refused to see Marcus. If truth be told, I was also lonely, in the evenings especially, and I felt sure speaking to Marcus again would, in some way, bring me closer to things as they once had been. Silly, really!

Pause

I don't know why I was so nervous on that Friday. I wondered if Victoria would be with him. I sincerely hoped so. Then again, I thought, she's such a chatterer, Victoria, totally monopolises any conversation and it always turns into a bit of a monologue about her latest leading man or some impertinent ingénue sleeping with her director. Also, she's always so chic — maybe on reflection it would be better if Marcus came alone.

Pause

I looked in the mirror on Friday morning and wasn't too impressed with the frumpy woman who stared back at me. Nothing merry about this widow, I thought. But why should there have been? I'd been standing at my husband's graveside a mere few days ago. Still, I didn't want to let Clifford down by looking too funereal and ancient. On impulse — for Clifford — I rang Jo in Hair Waves in Little Compton and at three o'clock I was having one of Jo's speciality blow dries. Stepping into my car an hour later I just happened to glance across at A La Mode and there, in the window, was a little gold and black top, just the type of thing I had been meaning to buy for some time to go with my long black skirt. I couldn't resist it. Perfect fit and the way they were able to match it with the new handbag, bracelet and earrings was most impressive. It's not a fashion shop I've used before — frightfully expensive — but I would certainly go back.

Pause

I had a quick bath when I got home and at six-thirty I looked in the mirror again. A big improvement! I thought I knew how Cinders must have felt before stepping into that transformed pumpkin. Yes, Marcus would have to be impressed. Not, of course, that I was in any way interested in his response. I knew that I had dressed up for Clifford, something I wish I had done more often in the past.

Pause

At a quarter to seven I wondered if Marcus would remember our— appointment. Where was he taking me? Where would we go? This was not a good idea. Wouldn't it be wonderful if he actually forgot or overlooked our da— arrangement. How much I could enjoy the peace of an evening on my own after such a rather frantic afternoon. I could finish my Antonia Fraser. I glanced in the mirror again. Too much lipstick, surely. I dabbed some off. I looked at my watch. It was seven

Act I

o'clock. The hall clock hadn't struck yet but it was always a few minutes slow before winding. He should have arrived.

Pause

"Please, Clifford, let your best friend not arrive," I prayed. And then I wondered, with a smile, if Clifford would, as yet, have attained a celestial position of such importance as to influence such social affairs.

Pause

He was now late. It was seven-o-two. I sat down and lifted *Marie Antoinette*. Only nineteen pages to read and he clearly wasn't going to arrive now. I didn't really feel like reading. I was much too nervous, nervous with annoyance, not anticipation, that was quite certain. How dare he make a — an appointment and fail to keep it! I glanced in the mirror again. I needed more lipstick. I rummaged in my new handbag. Such a beautiful accessory, now bought to no purpose. Twelve minutes past seven! It really was a frightful arrogance to fail to keep... I applied some of my newly bought lipstick, Mexican Midnight. Why, oh why had I ever consented to see this appalling Lothario so soon after... What a despicable person! The doorbell chimed.

Pause

I had no idea why, but my heart was pounding so loudly, I thought it must have been heard on the other side of the front door as I moved to open it. He was standing there, coatless, with a large bunch of carnations in his right hand. He leaned forward and pecked my cheek. "Millicent, my dear, not too late I hope?" "Not at all," I managed, smiling, "Is it seven o'clock yet?" "How wonderful you're looking," he beamed as he thrust the flowers towards me. "For me? How kind!" "Actually, they're not," he replied. "Could you get them into some water for me? They are for old Clifford. I thought we could go for a run up to the cemetery, this evening".

Lights cross-fade from Millicent to Dexie

Dexie It was no surprise to me when Fitz told me, eventually — I mean, I really had to drag it out of him — that he worked for MI7. I said I had never heard of that. MI5 and MI6, yes, I'd heard of them, but MI7, that was new to me. And he said, "Exactly, people don't know of us and that's the way it's meant to be. Security, my love, security! Now, no more questions or I'll have to start telling you lies." So we left it at that, but I did feel a bit of a tingle when I thought of us together. Me and this secretive, James Bond type man! It was only the day after when I suddenly thought, "I wonder if he's ever done for anyone?" You know, actually finished anybody off.

Pause

I couldn't put it out of my mind the rest of that day so I knew I would have to find out, somehow, the next time he came. It was usually Thursday or Friday nights that he called. He'd stay for an hour or so and occasionally stop over if he wasn't on an "engagement" as he called it.

Pause

After about six or seven weeks we began to fall into some sort of routine, I suppose. I really looked forward to seeing him. He was a right laugh most of the time. "How's my three favourite girls," he'd say as he looked into my eyes. "Sexy Dexie," then he'd drop his eyes, "Etna and Vesuvius?" Or "Dexie, Gert and Daisy?" Then he'd make a grab and his hands would be going all over and we'd be on the bed in seconds and I'd give him a real good time. He really enjoyed himself — and so did I. He was so different from all the others. After a couple of months I began to cut down on other punters — I didn't need them. Fitz insisted on me taking two hundred quid every visit — whether he stayed or not. Two hundred!

Pause

He never talked about his family. Few of them ever do. But I knew he was married. I don't know why but I just did. I don't mind that. The way I looked at it was like if he was perfect, happily married, he wouldn't be seeing me once, sometimes twice, a week, would he?

Pause

It must have been about four or five months after I first met him that I seen him as I had never seen before. He arrived with me at about three o'clock instead of the usual six-thirty, seven. I could see something was wrong. He was dead serious, no jokey hallo, nothing.

Act I 15

Never touched me, just sank down in a chair and asked for a drink. When I come back into the room, he had his head down in his hands and though he wasn't exactly sobbing, he was in tears. He had just heard, at lunch time, that one of his best mates had died. He was real cut up about it. I knelt down beside him, to comfort him "You mustn't upset yourself Fitz. It's…" "Oh for heavens sake stop calling me that stupid bloody name, my name's Marcus," he snapped. Got up, thumped his glass down on the table, slammed the door and was gone. He didn't call the next week, nor the next.

Lights cross-fade from Dexie to Victoria

Victoria People often ask, the media in particular, how one has kept married to the same man for so long. I mean, it was nineteen-sixty-five when Marcus and I tied the knot and forty-three years is a long — a very, very long — time in show business. I think it would be fair to claim that my reputation as an actress came from talent, not notoriety. I have never seen the attraction, for career or otherwise, in being photographed, semi-clothed or semi-conscious outside Carabelle's or La Petite Chatte at four o'clock in the morning. That should be the prerogative of aspiring page three tartlets or minor royalty learning their trade. Not of one looked up to as a role model by so many culture lovers not only in GB but further afield.

Pause

In the same way one keeps one's private life as private as possible. Whatever Marcus has got up to — and I'm quite sure there has been the occasional flirtatious glance — he has always been discreet... As I have been.

Pause

I suppose Clifford's death, when was it… ? He and Marcus were the same age and Clifford died at about forty-one or forty-two, so that would be round about nineteen seventy-nine or eighty. Immediately following that was a time when Marcus became very withdrawn and let his courtroom work envelop him. I rarely saw him for three or four months, but of course I was just finishing *Death in Florence*. Very Visconti-like but, sadly, dear Roger Regus was no Dirk Bogarde. Still he tried, poor dear, he tried — a little too hard, one felt. I mean really! No one should have to spend six months living penniless in a Sicilian mountain village with the goats to understand a part. One told him he should have just tried to act it. "It's a mercy," I said to him, "you were never cast as Jack the Ripper".

Pause

Yes, poor Marcus took Clifford's death very badly. But I felt it best to leave him to it. What's the current expression? "To give him some space." I knew the last thing Marcus would want, at that time of grieving, was a comforting female fluttering around muttering soothing platitudes. How ghastly!

Lights cross-fade from Victoria to Dexie

Dexie Just when I was quite sure I'd lost him, in he blows one Friday late afternoon. I say "lost him" because I didn't mind admitting I had grown to quite like him over those months. He was so different. So confident-like. Lovely clothes, shoes always polished, a real gent and we always had a laugh. He was generous too — but I told you that.

Pause

Anyway, in he blows about three or four weeks after his last stormy exit. "Did you miss me, girls?" he said with beaming grin. Then he grabs me, gets up to his old tricks again – which I didn't mind, cos I had missed him, and then we're lying there under my sheets and I decided to ask some questions. "Where was you?" "Don't ask, fair lady. You don't want to know." "I do want to know. Otherwise I wouldn't ask, would I? I know you was upset about your best mate but you've been gone a month. Why was that?" "Did you miss me?" he says. "Course I bloody missed you," I says and as soon as I'd said it I knew I shouldn't. Old Rose, who used to walk Ridgeway Road with me, when I was starting out, always told me, "First rule, my gal, don't get involved. Keep your feelings to yourself. It's your job, just your work. Do the business and keep your feelings for your old man and your kids when you have them." And here was me, telling Marcus Darcy, that I missed him. Old Rose would be wetting herself! "Well," he says, very quiet-like and he held up my chin with his hand and looked me straight in the eyes, "We'll have to do something about that Miss Doolittle." "And who's she when she's at home?" "Just another fair lady," he says. Then he springs off the bed into the bathroom and appears fully dressed, hair all combed, five minutes later. "Why are you rushing? Can't you stay?" I tried not to sound too pleading, "It's only five-fifteen". "I'm going to be very late. I need a peace offering,"

Act I

he says and suddenly he walks over to the window and grabs a big bunch of flowers — carnations they was — out of my black vase. I'd only got them from Angie that day. "These should do the trick. You don't mind, do you? I'll replace them." He slaps my money down on the table and opens the door. "But where are you going?" I cried, quite angry "Home?" "No, no," he said disappearing down the stairs, "perish the thought. Tonight I am hoping to start a new project. No rest for the wicked."

Lights cross-fade from Dexie to Millicent

Millicent I suppose, really, that's how it started — with a visit to the cemetery, where Marcus carefully placed the carnations on Clifford's grave, put a comforting arm around me and said, "Clifford, old man, permission to take your good lady out for the evening? We're missing you. Things aren't going to be the same but don't worry, I'll take good care of Millie. Rest easy, old man" and with that he armed me back to his car and said, "I meant that, Millie. I'd like to look after you now that Clifford can't. I know he would want that. Now what about a bite to eat? I've booked us a table at *The Hermitage*."

Pause

It was a delicious meal. Or maybe nervous apprehension had simply increased my appetite but I did enjoy it — after the first few minutes. Clifford and I didn't eat out all that much and I was not familiar with *The Hermitage* which was quite modern but very tastefully designed — nothing vulgar.

Pause

I'm more of a listener than a talker and Marcus must have recognized this for he did most of the talking. He wanted to know how I was coping and he wasn't hesitant about speaking of Clifford. Silly escapades from their Peterhouse years and one or two tales involving famous Petreans like James Mason, one of my favourite actors, and Thomas Gray, one of my favourite poets. I was fascinated, especially when he said that he used to be able to recite the entire *Elegy*. And then he said quietly, "Let me see, now".

Pause

"Full many a gem of purest ray serene
The dark unfathom'd caves of ocean bear
Full many a flower is born to blush unseen
And waste its sweetness on the desert air."

Pause

I don't know why but suddenly I knew I was blushing. I felt such a warm sensation spreading over my cheeks and neck. I tried to laugh and mutter "How clever!" but my mind was trying to analyze the significance of his quotation. Was I the unseen flower, wasted and unappreciated? Was he, the notorious womanizer, now going to ensure that I became better known? How did he plan to do that? How presumptuous of him — really — him of all people! I remembered Clifford's description, "a right randy old lecher" and here I was, dining with this very Casanova, giggling and blushing like a young thing.

Pause

The trouble was I felt like a young thing, not a widow who had just come from her husband's graveside. But I wasn't a dried up old prune, I reminded myself. I had not yet had my thirty-ninth birthday. I had a few more years of living to do. I was, if not beautiful, at least not unattractive. I enjoyed Jane Austen, Anthony Trollope, Wordsworth, Browning, Sibelius and Brahms and perhaps the *Mexican Midnight* was a mistake. I would ask, politely, but quite coolly, for Marcus to take me home immediately after coffee — and he would not be invited in for a nightcap.

Pause

Marcus was still talking as he spooned his way through a meringue and gooseberry fool. "Then after Oedipus and Ophelia came Plato and Polynices." "What on earth are you talking about?" I asked. "I thought I had lost you there for a moment or two. Got to keep up Millie. Our alphabetical succession of cats from our neighbours, the Mortons! He's classics master at St Anne's. Their cats are prolific breeders and he and his wife are for ever passing on their kittens — all classically christened — to any friends who will have them. Not a bad pudding that. Are you struggling?" "It was rather a large helping." Then he said "Do you know Susie Morton? Lovely gal, great sense of fun which her husband doesn't have. He's a dry old stick, as dry as she is — lively. But an entertaining couple, you'd like them — and you could

Act I

probably get a kitten. Lord, look at the time. We should go."

Pause

And before I had time to say a word, he was getting to his feet. "We'll be back in Chalfont St Clement in no time. Incidentally do you know who St Clement was?"

Pause

All the way back I kept thinking of Susie Morton — someone I didn't even know. Apart from the fact that she was — lively. I could believe it, with an equally "lively" neighbour like Marcus. What an impossible man he was! He hadn't mentioned Victoria nor his two young daughters, all night! When we reached home I was most definitely not going to invite him in.

Pause

Twenty minutes later we pulled up at my front door. It was quite dark. Marcus cut the engine. He leaned over towards me. I must confess my breath seemed to catch in my throat. He said, "Let's get your door open. Now, Millie, you'll not be offended if I don't come in but it's nearly midnight and Vicks worries if I'm late. You've been great company. I really enjoyed myself — and that is some shade of lipstick." And he was gone.

Pause

I locked and bolted the door and, passing, looked in the hall mirror. For some reason I seemed to be blushing again. And why I had some sort of strange empty feeling of disappointment, I had no idea. None at all. The *Mexican Midnight* still looked quite good, really. I might wear it the next time Marcus called. And I did, on so many occasions.

Lights cross-fade from Millicent to general dim Lighting

The three women are at their locations

Marcus, coated, in his 40's appears

Dexie When Marcus arrived with me late…

Marcus rushes across stage into her welcoming arms

and asked…
Marcus What's for supper?
Dexie (*to front*) I'd say (*to him*) "Me!"
Marcus (*in mock lecherous voice*) Yummy! Yummy!

They laugh, sweep and embrace

They run off

Millicent When Marcus arrived late at Chalfont St Clement.

Marcus appears and, while Millicent is speaking, takes off his coat as he walks to the coat stand, then neatly hangs it up

I'd say something like, "I've been listening to the Brahms number three. How was your day? And he'd ask…"
Marcus What's for supper?
Millicent What would you like, darling?
Marcus Right now, I'd like to take my cocoa, the crossword and old Brahms up to bed. Care to make it a threesome? (*Affectionately he kisses her on the cheek*)

They both smile as they exit arm in arm

Victoria When Marcus arrived home late…

Marcus enters and moves towards the third home base

I'd say, "Don't forget to lock up, Marcus" or he would! "I've had an impossible day. Absolutely fraught. Nigel's driver was late picking Barry and me up for the Aldwych and I had to restrain Barry from jolly well punching him."
Marcus Has Sandy left me anything for supper?
Victoria I've told Nigel before, Barry needs to be sent on an anger management course. And soon.
Marcus Bit of quiche, perhaps?
Victoria Don't be irritating, darling, go and see. You know I dislike trespassing in the kitchen. It's Sandy's domain. The annoying thing is Nigel just does not listen. How I am going to endure a run with Barry I do not know? Night, darling! (*She pouts her lips and makes a kissing sound to him*)

Act I

Victoria exits

Marcus watches her and smiles

Lights fade to Black-out

ACT II

Victoria You've probably all heard about the student at Uni, who writes home to her parents to say she's got engaged to a fifty-year-old Chinese chef who is a widower with six young children. She adds she is six months pregnant and she, her elderly fiancé and the six children are leaving to live in Hong Kong before the end of the month. Then she adds a PS, "This is all quite untrue but I have just failed both my chemistry and biology finals and will have to do re-sits. I just wanted you to get things in perspective, love, Susie."

Pause

All very amusing. Claudia didn't go to Sunderland Poly... Marcus finally put his foot down with considerable force and she went up to Cambridge — to Girton, to read Anglo Saxon, Norse and Celtic — a shade obscure but Claudia was never going to be predictable, as we were about to find out.

Pause

As she was coming to the end of the third term in her second year, we had a letter from her, which was unusual in itself, in that she usually phoned when she got in touch, which was not as often as it should have been. She would speak to Beatrice, or even to Sandy more often than she would do to her father or me.

Pause

I was in the middle of a very successful run with *Ghosts*, playing Mrs Alving, of course, with Julian, of all people, as my son, Oswald. You can imagine how we laughed at that casting. Wonderful notices, although everyone knew, I'm sure, that I was much too young for the part. Anyway, it was difficult for Claudia to speak to me during the run and Marcus, of course, was not often at home. So her letter arrived.

Pause

Act II 23

It was one of those moments — like hearing of the death of President Kennedy or of Princess Diana — when one remembers exactly what one was doing. I had just put the phone down, very excited, having been told by Oscar Lapoint about the proposed European tour of *Virginia Woolf,* beginning at the Salzburg Festival, maximum five performances per week — lovely — starting next June. Would I be interested? If not he would approach Rona's agent, Rona Magnus, that is. Now how delightful was that to hear — Oscar Lapoint choosing Rona, only if I were unavailable. He was such a perceptive director, despite his abortive experiment with the geriatric casting for *Salad Days*. A big, big no-no, I'm afraid.

Pause

So I had just replaced the phone — in the hall — when the letter slipped through the letterbox, alone. No other post. I recognized Claudia's flamboyant cursive instantly and I remember having an immediate premonition. Good news from Oscar, bad news from Claudia. Why is my daughter writing and not phoning. This is not good news. I knew it! Quite convinced! Nervously, very nervously — and I'm not generally a nervous person — I pulled those two pale green pages from their matching envelope. And at that moment my only thought was why Marcus is not here beside me, on this Saturday morning, instead of being at a conference in Edinburgh.

Lights cross-fade from Victoria to Dexie

Dexie I'd never been to Edinburgh before — never even been to Scotland but I wasn't going to see much of it, was I, no matter how much I'd have liked to see how different the shops was and so on. Everyone spoke with a Scottish accent, of course, but I could make them out all right most of the time and everyone in the hotel was smashing. Pampered me they did, but even when we was there two days I was still saying to Marcus, "This is crazy. I should be in London", and all he would say was "We are not going over all this again. We made our decision and we are sticking to it."

Pause

But it was his decision — not mine. I mean, I went along with it and the place he'd arranged for it was one of the poshest places I'd ever been in. And I could see, I suppose, why it would have been really difficult in London, with him always liable to be recognized. But it still seemed a bit extreme to me. I mean, why Edinburgh? What was wrong with Manchester or, better still, Liverpool? I would love to have seen the Cavern. Just to stand in it or even look at it from the outside and know that that was where such important music started out. But Marcus was determined, even when I put my strongest doubt in his mind, and I did, more than once. "Are you sure," I asked, "you want your son to be born a Scotsman?"

Lights cross-fade from Dexie to Victoria

Victoria More slowly this time I began to read the letter a second time. (*Producing it*) I've still got it, you see, after all these eighteen years. "Hallo Ma and Pa, Good news and glad tidings from your elder scion! I have become engaged to the most wonderful man and am leaving Girton at the end of this term. Pause for you to reach for the gin, Ma. You know that I have never been convinced about the ASNaC course and knowing that I am stopping it in a few weeks time has made me feel alive again! Julius is from Nigeria and he has been doing a post-grad year at King's in micro-engineering. He's frightfully bright and you will both love him."

Pause

"He has just accepted a new job in Paris, so we intend getting married there — how romantic is that, Ma — at the end of the summer. So in a few months' time — gosh it's so soon — your little girl will be Mrs Julius Kingdom Mbambo. Isn't that the most marvellous name! I want Beatrice to be bridesmaid, of course, and Julius wants you both to bring lots of friends over for a big splash weekend."

Pause

"He is hoping that lots of his own family will be there as well — he has eleven brothers and sisters and I'm still trying to learn all their names. He says, Pa, that you will have to give his family three cows or ten goats for them to give permission for Julius to marry me. Only joking! As well as being so good-looking, he has a great sense of humour and I think that's very important for a successful marriage, don't you?"

Pause

Act II

"I keep wondering what Miss Cheshire or little Miss Perdy would think of their ex-head girl's capture. My Julius! He'd make a great Othello, Ma. I'll phone you soon. Lots of love and kisses from us both, Your loving daughter and prospective son-in-law, Claudia and Julius."

Pause

My eye kept searching for the PS to say — "Not true, but I have failed my finals," etc., but it wasn't there. No post script. And no Marcus, poor darling! How would he react to this, I wondered. I would have to phone his hotel straightaway. At least, being at a conference, his mind would be on matters other than family.

Lights cross-fade from Victoria to Dexie

Dexie Our son was born at ten twenty-one on Saturday morning, the thirty first of May, nineteen ninety, weighing eight pounds, three ounces. He was perfect and seeing the look on Marcus's face as he cradled him in his arms for the first time was just magic. He grinned and cooed and let him look out of the window at the view — imagine — and then he became quite emotional. I'd never saw him like that before, really. He was the one who thought I shouldn't have it, when I first told him I was pregnant. Now look at him. The doting father or what, with tears in his eyes! To give him a laugh, I said, "Now then Daddy, I have definitely narrowed the name choice down to two. It's going to be Hamish or Jock!" And he laughed and I joined in — so much that the matron came in and when we told her she went off on one, as well. "My first husband," she laughed, "was called Hamish and he was from Sidcup".

Pause

When she left us — she was ever such a nice woman, what I would have liked my mum to be like, if I'd ever knew her. Well, when she went out, I took the baby back in my arms and Marcus sat on the edge of the bed and put his finger in the baby's little hand and that's when I told him. "It's going to be as you want, sweetheart. We're going to call him Clifford. But I want you in it as well, so, give Clifford Marcus a big kiss." And then, he really did cry.

Pause, as she remembers the moment

Then Mrs Alexander, the matron come in again to say the hotel had just phoned with an urgent message for Marcus. Would he please phone home immediately. Mrs Alexander gave us a strange look, I felt, as she said this. But quick as a flash Marcus said, "That will be from my mother. Always some sort of crisis when I'm away. Probably the ballcock in the downstairs loo playing up again." You could see why he was such a good barrister — so bloody quick.

Lights cross-fade from Dexie to Millicent

Millicent Gradually the visits from Marcus became more frequent, not, at the beginning, every week by any means, more like once every two or three weeks. It depended a lot on his other commitments and he did seem a very busy person. In fact that was one of the reasons for his more frequent visits. I began to do some secretarial work for him. Nothing important really, certainly nothing that he shouldn't have been able to have done in his chambers.

Pause

I think we both realized it was just an excuse to call with me but neither of us pretended that we thought this and things just developed from there. He would give me a ring and say, "If you have that statement proofed, I could call over this evening and pick it up. Seven thirty all right? Fancy a spot of dinner?" I never said no. In fact, I really looked forward to his coming. He was so dashing and so considerate — a really good friend.

Pause

It must have been after about six months, no, maybe less, when we arrived home after a wonderful meal at *The Hermitage* and two bottles of delicious Merlot. Marcus came in for coffee, as usual. He was taking the next day off work, he said, working from home, so he was in no hurry. He was so complimentary about how I looked and what I was wearing. "You know, Mills," he said. (No one else had ever shortened my name like that. Certainly not Clifford who always called me Millicent and wouldn't let anyone call me Millie, for instance.) "You know, Mills, you want to wear red more often. I've never seen you look so attractive. Yes, red is indisputably your colour. Damned alluring, Mills, if I may say so." Then he got up to go. "I'll see myself out." he said, gave me a peck on the cheek and the front door closed behind him.

Act II

Pause

Actually, being totally truthful, it wasn't exactly a peck on the cheek he gave me. With all that Merlot, it might well have been my fault, but I didn't manage to turn my cheek, it was my left — my left cheek — towards him quickly enough and, by mistake, it was more my lips he kissed. Quite accidentally, of course. Full on the lips.

Pause

Less than a minute later he knocked on the door and I opened it. "You'll not believe it. A front tyre as flat as the proverbial pancake. Have you got a garage number?" "At quarter to midnight, Marcus!" I said.

Pause

And that's how he came to spend the night in the guest room. Actually, being totally truthful, it wasn't exactly in the guest bedroom he spent the night. He did start helping me make up the bed there, that's true, but maybe with all that Merlot — well, anyway, I moved round to his side of the bed to straighten the valance and suddenly his hand was on my shoulder and very quietly — in almost a whisper really, I suppose you could say, certainly very sotto voce, he said, in my ear... my right ear, it was ... "Irresistible in red, Mills. It's the red cape makes the bull lose control. That long zip with the silver ring must slip down so easily, Mills." And it did.

Lights cross-fade from Millicent to Dexie, who has a glass in her hand, during most of her monologues from now on

Dexie I suppose I knew deep down that having a child with Marcus wasn't really going to make him spend a lot more time with me. In the first few months it did, a bit, but I took a long time to forgive him for rushing back to London the day after Clifford was born, leaving me alone in Scotland. Of course, the private nursing home was something else — a really smashing place and Mrs Alexander couldn't have done more for me. I mean, what did I know about looking after a new born baby but you learn quick when you've no alternative. And she was a good teacher.

Pause

Marcus phoned me every evening and insisted I stay in the home for the whole of the next week. Then he flew up to Scotland at the weekend and little Clifford and me flew back with him on Sunday to Heathrow. By that time I was more than ready to return home, to the two-bedroom semi that Marcus had bought for me — for us — in Ealing.

Pause

On the Monday morning, when he left, I don't think I've ever felt so alone and frightened. This little thing, crying a lot of the time, day and night, and only me to look after it! A twenty-four hours a day job and not just for a week or two. For five years at least, until he went to school. (*Refilling her glass*) It was Marcus, of course, who come up with the answer and over the next three or four months a string of nannies and au pairs came from two different agencies before finally I got one I liked and trusted. She was just like a younger version of Mrs Alexander, even down to the short hair cut, and there wasn't nothing she didn't know about new babies. Jean was her name and she came from Monday to Friday.

Pause

"A regime," I can still hear her saying, "you must get the baby into a regime." Marcus said she meant a routine, not a regime. I didn't care what she called it, but whatever it was it worked. Clifford began to do all the right things, eat or rather drink and sleep when he was supposed to and I was able to go up to town, walk around the shops again, have a coffee at my leisure, even try to look up Angie in "Fragrance and Flowers." But it had become a hairdressers and no-one there had ever heard of Angie.

Pause

Marcus would arrive at least once a week — even if only for an hour — depending on how busy he was. And the toys he bought for Clifford! I couldn't believe it. He was a very generous father and, of course, not only had he bought the house but he also opened a bank account for me and had money going into that every month. An unusual arrangement, I suppose you could say, but it was him insisted on the baby being born, and he knew I couldn't support a child on my own with no job of my own. So, there it was. It suited me and Marcus seemed happy. Jean was a diamond, though her hearing was going a little bit and suddenly Clifford was having his first birthday, then his second and third and life seemed very normal — except for one thing, and Marcus and me had many arguments about it. He was determined that Clifford must never know that he was Marcus's son. The word "daddy" never appeared in our little son's vocabulary.

Lights cross-fade from Dexie to Victoria

Victoria It was Beatrice who sent us the photographs of the wedding — not Claudia. I suppose that was understandable. Still resentful that we hadn't gone but it really would have been very difficult for me to fit it in with my rehearsal commitments for the BBC's *Black Cows on Monday* and as for her father, well, from the outset, from that never-to-be-forgotten phone call, when he arrived back from Scotland, he told Claudia she was making a ghastly mistake, throwing her life away, marriage was for life, impetuous actions are repented at leisure and so on. It was all very strong stuff delivered in his most masterful, persuasive Old Bailey manner. The only problem was that it wasn't some soft, woolly-brained, easily-impressed High Court Judge that Marcus was addressing. It was his own daughter and there is — and always has been — a steel in her genes, an unshakeable independence of spirit that makes her totally impervious to rational argument. Their brief conversation, was not, I'm afraid, conducted with any temperance of expression, by either party. Claudia gave as good as she got — oh yes!

Pause

I heard one or two unrepeatable suggestions bouncing out of the phone, mingled with choice phrases like "rotten bloody snob" and "disgusting racist" and "ashamed to be your daughter." It was all rather sad. Had we had time to become used to Claudia's decision, had she finished her degree, had she brought her young man to meet us — so many "if only's" but life isn't always as we want it to be, is it?

Pause

That phone call was the last time Marcus spoke to Claudia and I know it pained him very greatly. For Marcus, his elder daughter had always been the star in the family firmament, blessed with good looks, brains and personality. My goodness, she even played the role of a bald, middle-aged tramp in her school play and was totally convincing! What could she not have achieved intellectually, artistically? "What a waste! What a bloody waste!" was his heart-broken comment, so often made to me in private.

Pause

It even affected his attitude to Beatrice, poor lamb. Beattie was never going to be another Claudia but she did try so hard. From her earliest days one could see how much Beattie idealized her sister. But she hadn't her looks, she was always an awkward child, very gauche in her teenage years and, I'm afraid, not overly blessed academically. She auditioned every year for a part in the school play — always without success. She was never selected for a lacrosse or hockey team and, embarrassingly, at the gymkhana, she spent more time on the floor than on her pony. I fear she was often the butt of her peers' rather malicious, teenage humour and she had no really close friend. However, she did have one quality that neither Claudia nor her father had. A gentleness and kindness of spirit that always put consideration of others before herself. I'm not sure whether she took that entirely from me.

Pause

Marcus did not even glance at the wedding photographs — at least not in my presence. They were certainly colourful; every colour, bright gaudy colour, that is, that you could imagine. Red, green, yellow, blue, orange splashed across every shot and so, so many people with wide smiles — lots of teeth in every photograph. It looked to me like a mini Notting Hill Carnival. And I don't think I have ever seen so many children all immaculately dressed, the boys all attired in three piece suits and cravats. The noise at the reception, where, Beatrice informed us, there was an eight piece steel band, must have been too brutal to imagine. I kept two of the photographs. One of Claudia, looking quite radiant, alone with her smiling husband and the other of Claudia and Beatrice on their own. Both looked very happy. (*Pause*; *taking a photograph out of a bag and looking at it*) As it turned out, Beatrice tells us Claudia is very contented, serenely happy. She has moved home twice, now living somewhere on the outskirts of Bordeaux. She has five children, four girls and a boy and, again according to Beatrice, has become "quite plump". For Beattie to use that terminology must mean that Claudia has become very fat indeed. (*Pause*) I would like to see our grandchildren. Actually, the eldest girl is called Victoria Regina, but Marcus — well... It's not easy —life can't always be as one wants it. "Slings and arrows of outrageous

Act II   31

fortune" and all that!

Lights cross-fade from Victoria to Millicent

Millicent That night, that first night with Marcus, was, without any shadow of doubt whatsoever, the most exciting, most wonderful night of my life. I had never before — shared a bed, with any man in my life, apart from my husband, and Clifford and Marcus, the closest of friends, were two very different men. Please don't misunderstand me. I loved my husband totally as I believe he did me but our time together was one of comfort, a caring companionship, sedate and entirely predictable. We both seemed to enjoy it that way, indeed I could not have imagined it otherwise. There were no children, for reasons that I feel it unnecessary to talk about and our marriage sailed serenely on, until that shocking day when he passed away last year.

Pause

Clifford was not an amorous man, certainly not a passionate one — it simply wasn't in his nature. Looking back I can see now why I often thought of him as a brother or as a very close friend rather than as a lover. I know he loved me but I think he had a deeper love, a truer love, but one that was unrequited. It was a love that he couldn't help — that went back to his schooldays and continued through university. And I know that not for one second did Marcus know anything about it.

Pause

When Marcus was leaving that following morning, I followed him as he rushed down the stairs, no time for breakfast. "What about your flat tyre?" I called. "Don't you know," he smiled, "about the power of positive thinking. I guarantee that tyre will have repaired itself." And it had — not, I must admit, that I was at all surprised! Now, could you imagine Clifford behaving like that?

Lights cross-fade from Millicent to Dexie

Dexie I met Cecil Batch in *The Leaping Lady* one Friday night when Marcus had promised to call and hadn't. It was nearly a fortnight since I seen him and I knew why. For the last few months we'd been having one hell of a ding-dong over Clifford and his future education. He was now seven and going to private day prep, fees, of course, paid by his father, Uncle Marcus! Now, his loving father wanted to send our only child to boarding school and Jean and me wasn't having it.

Pause

I'd spotted him before, always on his own, in the corner opposite the darts board corner, beside the door to the toilets. I caught him looking at me once or twice, and gave him a bit of a smile — not much, not enough to say "What's keeping you?" but enough to show I didn't mind him looking.

Pause

On the second or third night I seen him, he comes up to the bar where I was ordering and having a natter with Gerry, the owner, and he says, "Good evening, unpleasant weather." It was hardly the most original chat up line I ever heard, but Cecil wasn't your normal chat-up artist as I found out. Even the look of him was different. About five foot eight, polka-dot tie, sports coat and grey flannels — a throwback to the fifties, I thought. We done the weather bit and then he says "May I buy you a drink?" and who was I to refuse a gentleman's kind offer, specially when my own gentleman was playing silly buggers at the time. I can honestly say I never looked at another man — well, maybe looked, but that was all — since Marcus and me got together. But, I dunno, maybe it was some sort of seven year itch thing. Anyhow, I wasn't seeing as much of Marcus now as I wanted to and I always did like a bit of male company. Jean was about most of the time, 'cept for weekends, but that was different and her hearing was playing her up bad.

Pause

When I thought back to the first five years and the Dublin weekends, those was great times — "Rare Ould Times" as we sang so often, in so many pubs. We used to fly over on a Friday night and have a wild weekend. Marcus could really let his hair down, in a different country where the chances of him being recognized was small. I'll never ever forget those Dublin weekends. We must have visited every pub in the centre of Dublin and along the quays. Drinking and singing all the pop songs — non-stop. Everyone knew all the words, that's what got me, whether it was Tom Jones, the Beatles, Sandy Shaw, Englebert, they all knew them. And there would Markie be, in the middle of the floor, open-necked shirt, sleeves rolled up, head back, red-faced, sweat pouring off him, a pint of Guinness in his hand,

Act II

belting out *Is This the Way to Amarillo?* and I never seen him so happy. Sometimes there'd be a ceilidh band in the corner and we'd be stamping out feet in time and clapping our hands and someone would pull you out on to the floor and you could hardly see through the cigarette smoke and you'd whirl round with your partner, making arches, spinning round, then making a wave to advance on another wave, duck under them and the insistent beat drove you on until you collapsed in each other's arms at the end and a great cheer would go up. That was "the craic" every night and they used to say "The craic was mighty." (*Pause*) The craic was mighty. Yeah, it was.

Pause

When last did Markie and me have a "mighty" night? So long ago I couldn't remember. Polka Dot was peering at me, over his glasses, having just asked me a question. "Sorry?" I said. "Your name," he said, "I was just asking ..." "Debbie," I replied "and yours?" "Cecil, he said, "Cecil Batch. No "elor". "Sorry?" "Just Batch — not Batch-elor." He chuckled and I — joined in! To-night, I thought, the craic is not going to be mighty!

Lights cross-fade from Dexie to Victoria

Victoria So, you know about Claudia and — her husband and children in France. You also know of Marcus' busy life, leading in some very high profile cases. The Derbyshires was such a strain over six months, but such a high profile triumph for him in the end. Then the travelling to conferences, to lecture — such a hectic schedule. He claims he is almost as busy as I am.

Pause

I must admit the last RSC season went spectacularly well — what a splendid role Volumnia is! I mean yes, she is proud and power-hungry, domineering, cold-blooded and calculating, not easy for me to play, as Barry said, but I think I made the audience like me, just a little bit. And what an unexpected hit *Black Cows on Monday* has become — now in its third series. I heard through the grapevine — actually from one of the script writer's many boyfriends — he has quite a few — that my character, Aunt Isabel, was to be written out in the last episode. She was supposed to fall down a well! Now a car crash I would not mind. A terminal illness would also be quite acceptable but I was determined that Aunt Isabel would not depart this life via a disused farmyard well. There must be some dignity in passing on — even in a TV soap. So I have notified the producer that due to other pressing commitments I shall be unavailable for the fourth series and accordingly I would expect an appropriate exit episode. He did not look as upset as I'm sure he was feeling. After all, who did he think was maintaining his ratings, week after week.

Pause

Now that leaves only Beatrice to tell you about. And some surprising and really rather inspiring news there. Last year, at the age of thirty-four, Beatrice was married to the Reverend Arthur Ferrisby, a Church of England vicar with a church somewhere near Shepton Mallet. Now you have probably seen, all too often, the rather silly caricature of the local vicar, portrayed by, for example, Derek Nimmo — all fluttering hands, perpetual smile, and rather thin, weedy voice. So unfair and so exaggerated I always thought — until I met Arthur. Clearly, Derek Nimmo had based his character exactly on Arthur — vague, disorganized, totally not of this world, but a delightful, sensitive soul really. He is fifteen years older than Beatrice and he was married before. Marcus had a rather lengthy interrogation of the poor man. He was so nervous when he came to ask for Beatrice's hand in marriage — so old-fashioned yet so engaging.

Pause

Marcus was really rather naughty with him. When Arthur asked, as he did, for Beatrice's hand, Marcus, who had had a few drinks that afternoon, said "One hand won't be much use to you, Vicar, take the whole package. She's yours, legs, feet, the lot. By the way, no cows or goats required?" I confess I was listening outside the study door and when I heard that I rushed into the room, on some pretext. In that impish frame of mind, Marcus could easily have put the dear man off. But Arthur seemed quite calm, if rather bemused, and I explained that the reference to livestock was an obscure family joke. He insisted on telling us that his first wife, Muriel, had left him after just ten months of marriage, running off with a campanologist from a neighbouring parish. After he had gone, with our consent, of course, Marcus made some sixth form comments about poor old Arthur not ringing Muriel's bell and wondering how our little Beatrice would find life on Mars, etc. — all very juvenile but really quite funny. We stood in the kitchen, drank a full bottle of Sauvignon and howled with laughter. "We've had the carnival with Claudia, now for the Whitehall farce with

Act II

Beatrice," he roared. No one could ever make me laugh like Marcus.

Lights cross-fade to Millicent

Millicent It seemed the most natural thing in the world to say yes when Marcus asked me to become his PA, looking after all his travel commitments in particular and accompanying him every time he left London. Throughout the eighties and nineties were wonderful years. As a leading authority on criminal law, procedure and punishment he was much in demand as guest speaker at seminars, conferences and congresses throughout the world.

Pause

I found it all quite fascinating. It was such a new world to me and I could well understand the frustrations Marcus so frequently felt as he spent long hours trying to coordinate diverse legal niceties and practices from members of the UN to gain acceptance as statute for the International Criminal Court. His fiery disputes over the draconian views of the Hon. Justice Bernard Lamming-Jones and indeed with the Attorney General, himself, made him very controversial. But Marcus would tilt at any windmills, particularly established ones. Some of his speeches were quite remarkable even to a lay person such as I. So passionate and so eloquent!

Pause

I often wondered, as I waited for him in my hotel room in Geneva or Stockholm or Adelaide, why I could feel no guilt at being his mistress. For that's what I was primarily. His staff in his chambers could have booked flights, corresponded with hosting organizations, typed speeches and such like. But we both knew that my role carried further ministrations and we were both so joyously happy with that.

Pause

How could I feel guilt being with the man I loved as I had never loved before and who returned that love so manifestly. My husband was dead so I was free and Marcus... Well, Victoria was scarcely the adoring wife. I remembered Clifford's words, "Don't underestimate Vicks... more than a match for old Mar."

Pause

She had her own career and was so talented, but being the loving wife, looking after her husband did not seem to interest her greatly. Not a role she seemed anxious to play.

Pause

In a strange way I sometimes felt that in loving Marcus I was fulfilling a missing part of Clifford's life. For as I reflected upon my marriage, more and more I became convinced that my gentle, self-effacing husband, whom I had loved totally, had chosen the wrong partner in life and I could see, so easily, how the magnetism of Marcus' personality could attract the adoration of either man or woman.

Pause

In the evening after supper we would often stroll, arm in arm, along unfamiliar streets, always to end up in a tavern of some kind, where the re-action of Marcus would invariably be the same — "A very tame establishment, no life, needs a bit of a sing-song", and I would say "Don't be silly, Marcus. People are here to drink and talk, not to sing harri-koke, or whatever it's called."

Pause

It was the adrenaline, you see, still pumping after his day's activity. He didn't really want to jump up and sing in exhibitionist style. No, no! He was quite happy to sip his glass of wine with me. He just didn't always realize that.

Lights cross-fade from Millicent to Dexie

Dexie (*with a glass, drinking*) Cecil mightn't of been the best company in the world but at least he was company. We would meet up most nights in *The Lady* and he was always glad to see me, a little port or vodka waiting for me on the little round table for two near the toilets. I liked to see his eyes light up when I come through the door. I really meant something to him. That felt good and he was never no trouble about anything. Whatever I said, he was happy. Even when Gerry, he was the barman, or Maisie, his wife, always wore white, she did, behind the bar — even when one of them said "That's it, luv, you've 'ad enough", and I got a bit funny about it, as you do. Cecil would be over, quietly moving me — sometimes bloody pulling me — back to the table, coat on and we was out of there before I knew. You need a

Act II

friend like that with you, when you think you is OK, compis mental and all that, but you have had a bit of a skinful really and everything is swaying a bit.

Pause

Don't get me wrong. That wasn't every night it happened — I was never banned from T*he Lady* or nothing like that, like I was from *The Derby Arms*, but sometimes — I dunno — sometimes, like, you felt so bloody depressed and a few quick double vodka made you relaxed again and I could forget about His Worship for a while. Fact is I miss Jean more than His Worship. Mind, I didn't miss the way she looked at me when Cecil helped me in most nights. Her face was always so — so — disa... Not liking what I was becoming, that sort of look... You know what I'm trying to say. "Don't wake the child," she'd always say, like a bloody record, "don't wake the child" as me and Cecil went up the stairs. But Cliffie boy, my beautiful son, always slept like a log. He was a lovely boy and so smart.

Pause

That's the only reason Markie ever called now — to spend time with Cliffie, not with me. We had some awful rows, Marcus and me. Always about my drinking. He'd say, "Stop this destructive drinking, woman. Look at what you're doing to yourself. Look at what you've got." "That's my problem, Marcus. I am looking at what I've got and what have I got?" "You've got a house, a good home, a housekeeper and a fine son you should be proud of." "I am proud of him. And so should you Marcus. You should be his father instead of his uncle. It's pathetic."

Pause

And that would end it. He'd walk away. And when he shouted about what I'd got, I really wanted to say the only thing I really wanted, the only thing I couldn't have, was him.

Pause

And Clifford, my beautiful boy, I was going to lose him too. Marcus arrived one night unexpectedly, otherwise I wouldn't have had Cecil there. Jean had left me a few weeks before and he stormed in. He had his own key and he didn't like what he seen. He grabbed poor

Cecil and threw him, his jacket and his trousers into the front garden, emptied two bottles — luckily not full — down the kitchen sink and then said "any doubt I might have had is now removed" and Clifford was definitely going to boarding school in September. "I can lose you," he shouted "but I will not lose my son." And I couldn't think straight to argue. But I knew then I had lost Marcus for good.

Lights cross-fade from Dexie to Victoria

Victoria About two or three years after we were married, certainly before Claudia was born, so it must have been about nineteen sixty-seven or sixty-eight, Marcus took me to New York for a birthday treat. We saw two Broadway shows which were rather unremarkable, but we went to Sardi's after one of them, and I think that's where we saw Fred Astaire and Ginger Rogers. A pleasant little man he seemed to be but I thought she looked much better on screen. However, the really memorable event for both Marcus and me was when we managed to get two seats for an Ella Fitzgerald concert. She was then about fifty but what a divine voice. (*She sings the first line of a well known Ella Fitzgerald song*) We were both mesmerized. And when she finished with... (*She sings the final line of the same song*) ...and we were clapping furiously, Marcus squeezed my arm and whispered "How about it? I'll watch over you if you'll watch over me." So silly really, but it was such a sentimental moment. No one could say Marcus was ever "A little lamb lost in the wood" — a wily old fox, maybe, but a lost lamb — I don't think so. Now why was I telling you about that? Oh, yes. (*She remembers*)

Lights cross-fade from Victoria to Millicent

Millicent I was out with Cecil, in the village, our usual walk — I don't believe I told you about Cecil, not that there's much to tell. Some months ago, Slipper, my darling black Labrador had to be put down. Old age, I'm afraid, with all its ghastly canine consequences and the vet, an old friend, said it would be best for Slipper. So one Friday afternoon, Marcus took Slipper away and I was most upset.

Pause

A week later Marcus arrived one evening and in the back of the car he had the most adorable little Labrador pup, black as your boot. "For you," he said, "a new Rottweiler for Madame. Don't go too close. He'll rip your hand off."

Act II

Pause

We took him in and that's when Marcus made his strange request. He very much wanted to train it himself and to call it, Cecil. "But you can't call a dog, Cecil," I said. "Why not?" was the response I got. It was a fine old English name — going back to the Domesday Book and beyond. Cecil was a noble, distinguished name — "Just right for a dog," he declared, rather forcefully I thought. So, Cecil it was.

Pause

And several days later, when Cecil was old enough, Marcus was as good as his word and Cecil began his training to walk at heel, to roll over, to play dead, to hold position until Marcus released him and so on. It was all most impressive. Marcus would shout "You're dead, Cecil" and down the little chap would go, still as could be, scarcely breathing. He seemed to get enormous pleasure from this — Marcus, that is, not the dog.

Pause

So I was taking Cecil for his walk through the village, saw the card stand outside Mitchell's and suddenly a thought struck me. It's going to be Marcus's sixtieth in the summer. I wonder was Victoria planning anything. I should ring her.

Lights cross-fade from Millicent to Victoria

Victoria It was after the wedding, the next day. Beatrice and Arthur had already left on their honeymoon to the Orkneys, yes, the Orkneys! Arthur had done a theological thesis, at some time or other, on a very large church there, in fact a cathedral, I think — St Magnus, possibly an early ancestor of Rona, I thought!

Pause

Apparently it is a most impressive architectural piece of twelfth century building, and Arthur, as a visiting young curate, quite fell in love with it. So he couldn't wait to take his new bride to see it and apparently the bracing Orcadian air is also very soothing on Arthur's eczema and hives, but more about the wedding in a moment.

Pause

When Marcus and I came down to breakfast in the hotel the next morning, after the wedding, Claudia and Julius were just finishing and Claudia was waving some tickets in the air. It appeared that dear Beatie, ever thinking of others, had booked four theatre tickets for us to go to a performance that very evening.

Pause

She had left Marcus and me a letter. (*Producing it*) "Dear Ma and Pa, Our heartfelt thanks for giving Arthur and me such a memorable day — one we shall both treasure all our lives." She goes on... well, I needn't read you all of it... She's such a grateful girl... such gratifying words for one to read... Anyway, here we are... "Now about the tickets. You will remember, Pa, how upset you were to miss seeing Claudia in that three-man play at school, directed by little Miss Perdy — remember her, Ma? — so long ago. When I saw another, new three-man play, was running at the Bristol Vic, I thought it such a coincidence that I just had to buy you tickets so that you could all go together as you had not been able to before. Claudia will not be appearing in it, but she will be sitting with you, and Ma, you will not mind a busman's holiday, I hope. The theatre will make a great fuss about you being there I'm sure. Please enjoy it."

Pause

Wasn't that sweet? Marcus began to huff and puff when I read this out to him but when I told him what this new play was called, all threatened objections ceased and we all went to see the very moving *Someone Who'll Watch Over Me*.

Lights cross-fade from Victoria to Millicent

Millicent   The wedding of Beatrice and Arthur was delightful. Low key, but that was the way both wanted it, much to Victoria's disappointment. She would have booked the Abbey had she had her way, but it was so good to see Beatrice asserting some independence and having the occasion as she wished it.

Pause

Of course, it meant us all being whisked west to Somerset, to Arthur's parish, to a bijou little sandstone church like something out of *Alice in Wonderland*.

Act II

Pause

Victoria and I had made one or two preliminary visits checking on seating, floral arrangements, catering etc. It was a good job Marcus asked me to accompany Victoria. She is so indecisive and such a fusser. She had the little caretaker, Albert, demented. Such a helpful little man — he had a most frightful limp and hobbled up and down the aisle with his big, soulful eyes, like a bloodhound, looking over at me for help. "This can't possibly be all the light. It's so dark. Try the balcony lights too." And off he would scurry. "No, no that's hopeless. My daughter cannot be married in such Stygian gloom. Haven't you more candles?" Scurry, scurry, scurry. "Marginally better. At least we shall see the main protagonists but just look at the shadow now falling across that front pew. I cannot possibly sit in shadow. Guests will want to see the bride's mother. Now look, Albert, you sit there." And she grabbed little Albert by the shoulders and seated him, like a recalcitrant Joyce Grenfell infant, in the front pew. "Now don't you see what I mean, you've almost gone from view. You must feel like Osvald – do you know Ibsen's *Ghosts*, Albert? – crying out, "The sun, mother, give me the sun."

Pause

I'm afraid at that stage I intervened firmly. "Victoria," I said, "Albert cannot give you the sun. He has given you everything he can and I know you are so grateful to him. What would we have done without him? The light is so perfect, so atmospheric — not ideal for *Oklahoma*, I grant you, but just right for a refined wedding." That seemed to settle it, and I noticed out of the corner of my eye, Victoria passing Albert a twenty pound note as we left the church. I would not swear to it, but I think I also heard an urgent aside, "More candles, Albert."

Pause

To my great surprise and delight, Claudia and her husband, Julius, with little Victoria Regina, all arrived for Beatrice's big day. I scarcely recognized Claudia — she had put on so much weight — but she flung her arms around me. "Aunt Mills, how wonderful to see you again," and the same vivacious, dynamic personality was just as always. Her husband was equally delightful. Charming, erudite and so relaxed, Julius soon had his parents-in-law in the palm of his hand. It was quite a performance — no, not a performance for Julius seemed totally natural and sincere. He was all that Beatrice had told her parents he was and he clearly worshiped Claudia. They were a sparkling couple and little Victoria Regina, V.R., as they called her, was adorable.

Pause

Obviously I did not see it, but Marcus told me later, that he and Julius spent quite a bit of time together — they even went, as a foursome, to see a play in Bristol. Marcus said to me, "Not exactly my idea of an entertaining evening, spending it in the company of three hostages shackled to three radiators in a cell in Beirut. It's a long story but I wouldn't have been there if I hadn't been with you, on our first evening at *The Hermitage*, many moons ago. Do you remember?"

Pause

Of course I did. What I also remember feeling at that wedding, were definite stirrings of guilt, seeing Marcus with Victoria and his family, so happy, so together. I could very easily, at that moment, have taken a taxi to the station and made my way back to Chalfont, to the reality of my own loneliness with a black Labrador my only friend. Oh what a tangled web we weave...

Lights cross-fade from Millicent to Victoria

Victoria Coming up to Marcus' sixtieth I rang his PA, Millicent, or she rang me. I can't recall exactly. Anyway it didn't matter which. She's frighteningly efficient, lives on her own, since her husband, Clifford, died, in their old Victorian house buried somewhere in Surrey. Marcus takes her on the occasional trip, although he finds her a bit of a dry old stick — kindly and meticulous but so dull. "How would you like to arrange a party?" I asked.

Lights cross-fade from Victoria to Millicent

Millicent I got home from my constitutional, fed Cecil and finally decided to contact Victoria, which is never easy. I spoke to the housekeeper, Mrs Sanders and found out that Victoria would be at home the following day till lunchtime, then at the television studio until "much too late to take a call."

Pause

Act II   43

However I did speak to Victoria the next morning and, as I half expected, she had forgotten all about it. "His sixtieth?" she queried, "Surely not. I can't be as ancient as that. Oh, Millicent, you are a treasure! What would we do without you? Now, what are you thinking of? The Ritz, the Savoy or the Connaught?"

Lights cross-fade from Millicent to Dexie

Dexie There was one thing I was certain about. If His Lordship was having a birthday bash, two of the people not on the menu or not on the guest thingy, would be his only son and his only son's mother. That didn't seem right to me... not to be invited. The question was what to do about it.

Lights cross-fade from Dexie to Millicent

Millicent Of course, in the end, I had to have a word with Marcus because Victoria and I simply could not agree.

Pause

As I expected Marcus and I were of one mind, our thinking is invariable alike! If he had to have a party at all, and he knew that Victoria would insist upon it, it would be at home. "You know why Vicks is thinking of a venue in the city, don't you? To have a red carpet, paparazzi and turn it into a bloody Oscars ceremony. No thank you." So Chessley Park it was. Marquee on the front lawn, outside caterers, one to one hundred and fifty guests, Humphrey Lyttelton, Kenny Ball or Acker Bilk for music from ten to two a.m. All quite straight forward, even down to a list of twenty not to be invited! *Personae very non gratae!*

Lights cross-fade from Millicent to Victoria

Victoria Although Millicent seemed very keen on the Connaught, I really felt that a more discreet occasion, here at home, would appeal to Marcus much more. Neither of us is too keen on the limelight, despite my celebrity, and whilst one could tolerate the publicity if one were forced to, I had to insist that Millicent should plan for a more homely party. The Windsors are so often a problem! I entirely agreed with Marcus however. If one cannot have the first division, one does not want minor royalty — more trouble than they are worth what with drains being lifted, security men in every hydrangea and sniffer dogs in every drawer. Sandy wouldn't have it.

Lights cross-fade from Victoria to Dexie

Dexie It was a phone call from Clifford — he was settling in so well — that inspired me, I think. He was chatting on about how the boys in his dormitory had formed into two gangs, the Apaches and the Sioux, and he was an Apache. They had each took a motto, he said. The Sioux motto was in Latin, about the stars, "astra" or something. I didn't understand it all — we was a bit short on Latin learning at St Emilia's Primary School, proper English was a big enough struggle for most of us — but it sounded like "pear hardo aster" — something like that and it meant it was hard to get up to the stars.

Pause

The Apache thingy was easier – "Who dares wins." All the boys in the Apaches liked that, apart from Sebastian Weinberger who was a total cry baby and wouldn't take part in the blood-brothers' ceremony at midnight in the Juniors' locker room. "We have secret passwords," whispered Clifford, "but I can't tell you them or I will have all my toes cut off. I shouldn't even be telling you this much. Promise you won't tell anyone." So I promised. Who would want a toeless ten-year-old?

Lights cross-fade from Dexie to Victoria

Victoria I simply could not decide about Terrence Magnus. Rona told me she hadn't seen him for six months — probably an exaggeration — but I had heard that he was playing up again — shaven head, orange toga and handing out leaflets on the Piccadilly line. Naturally I thought these would be of a religious nature but apparently not. They were advertising half-price pizzas in a kebab shop in Cockfosters.

Pause

Still, he was Rona's husband — her third — and it would seem strange to invite her on her own. On the other hand, having a deranged, orange-robed pizza promoter at Chessley was a risk I was not prepared to take.

Lights cross-fade from Victoria to Millicent

Act II

Millicent Perfect! Over one hundred acceptances already. Marquee, band, catering all arranged. Weather forecast excellent. Victoria's excesses kept reasonably under control — apart from the floral extravaganza — and for me, a new pair of red and black shoes exactly matching my red dress. Perfect! It would be a wonderful occasion.

Light cross-fade from Millicent to Dexie

Dexie "Who dares wins!" The Apache's motto kept ringing in my head long after I'd put the phone down. It was almost like a call to action had been sent to me and by Markie's own son. OK, you haven't been invited to the birthday bash but that don't mean you can't go. Be bold. Take the initiative, like I keep telling poor Cecil. "Who dares wins!" And it's tomorrow night, according to the housekeeper, Mrs Sanders, who I had heard all about the party from when I phoned, putting on a posh voice, to speak to Markie some weeks before. Very uppity she sounded. "If it's about Sir Marcus's forthcoming birthday party, his PA is handling all calls." That would be old Milly that Markie had told me about.

Pause

That night in bed I suddenly turned to Cecil. "How would you like to go to a party — free eats, plenty of booze?" "At Gerry and Maisie's?" he asks. "Not exactly," I said.

Lights cross-fade from Dexie to Victoria

Victoria Half-a-hour to curtain and all in order. The grounds look magnificent and the house, itself, quite splendid. I have never seen the antique furniture looking quite so well, such splendid props, the mahogany, tambour-top writing desk — Marcus's favourite — and the matching mahogany and sabicu lady's writing cabinet — my favourite. We should start to use them some day.

Pause

Now who will arrive first? None of my professional colleagues, I'm afraid. One needs an audience to make a proper entrance. I do hope Sandy has got over her little tantrum with the caterers. Who's worried about the temperature of the pâté on such an evening?

Lights cross-fade from Victoria to Millicent

Millicent (*posing, as if looking in full length mirror*) Yes, though I say it myself — just as perfect as I can make it. I want to look so right for Marcus. He always looks so magnificent in black tie.

Pause

For old times sake, I've resurrected the *Mexican Midnight*.

Lights cross-fade from Millicent to Dexie

Dexie We was in *The Leaping Lady* from about seven-thirty p.m. and I still hadn't decided for sure. Cecil had borrowed his uncle Fred's old Mazda, just in case, and I didn't let him drink, just in case. Maisie knew something was up. "Where you going, girl? Proper smart you're looking — real fancy." I said we was invited to a party but we wasn't sure we was going yet. "Blimey, pity to waste that little outfit on Gerry and me. He's seeing more of you tonight, peeping out of that dress than he's ever seen before. Ain't that right, Gerry!" And she was right. I was looking good — even Cecil said so. "Never seen your skirt so short before. A real *mini* mini," he says. I always had good legs so, why not show 'em. That's what I think.

Pause

At about ten o'clock, as Gerry is putting another brandy and ginger in front of me, he says, "Heard from the lad lately?" Suddenly I could hear Clifford's voice, clear as if he was beside me "The Apaches and the Sioux. Who dares wins, Mum." He's telling me what to do, and I needed that guidance. I look at Cecil. "Drink up, Cec. We're going for a drive in the Mazda."

Lights cross-fade from Dexie to Victoria

Victoria First to arrive? Dear Millicent, of course. Fluttering around everything and everywhere. Looking rather obvious in a startling red outfit that would have looked old-fashioned on her grandmother. She reminded me, poor darling, of a frenetic fire engine out of control. But a lovely smile. "Millicent, darling, how divine you look and what a dress! Gucci or Givenchy?"

Lights cross-fade from Victoria to Dexie

Dexie We drove through the gates of Chessley Park shortly before

Act II

47

midnight. There was no trouble finding the village and once there we could hear the noise of the band.

Pause

I never seen such a mansion and such grounds before, except in the cinema. Massive they was. Driving up the avenue there was little lamps or light thingies on either side of the driveway, lovely bushes of all shapes, with the headlights picking up all the different flowers on them. The music was getting louder as we drove up. Cecil says, "Are you sure about this?" I didn't say anything, but I was thinking, "This could have been Clifford's home — and maybe mine."

Pause

Suddenly we see this huge house over to our right, all spotlit with cars parked along its side. In front of the house was a big grassy park-land area and at the end of it a big white tent — like a circus top almost, but the sides was all tied up so you could see right inside. Hundreds of people, I would say, was sitting at tables, drinking or dancing to a band that was on a built-up platform place. The loudspeakers was blasting out the music. No one was eating, for a whole squad of waiters and waitresses, all in green and black uniforms, was buzzing back and forward taking empty dishes around the back of the house.

Pause

The noise, the laughter — it sounded as if everyone was having a good time, a good party time. We parked where a man with a yellow jacket on directed us and then me and Cecil got out of the car and locked it. The guard said, "Good evening Sir, Madam" and touched his forehead.

Lights cross-fade from Dexie to Millicent

Millicent The parking worked out exactly as I had planned it and we didn't need to use the lower meadow after all. Still it was a sensible precaution. The flow of people also went as planned. Marcus and Victoria receiving guests in the hallway, Beatrice and I moving them quickly into the library for their drinks, on into Marcus' study, through the french window and out across the front lawn and down to the tables at the marquee. Of course, some tried to stand and talk in the library or start admiring the books but I was quite firm — polite, of course — but quite determined to keep them moving. Just sheep, really, most of them, especially the politicians – dim sheep!

Pause

Until we actually heard them we were all a bit concerned about the band but within a few minutes of their starting to play, I knew the agent had been correct. We had a winner! In fact I heard one bejewelled female announce to her group, "I only want to go to heaven if Mitch Mills and his Swanee Six Jazzmen are there to greet me at the pearly gates." Really! I wondered if she'd ever heard a *Sibelius* Symphony?

Lights cross-fade from Millicent to Victoria

Victoria All went so very, very well. The number of compliments I received about my little "M & S number", as I called it, were countless; and the tiara drew a great deal of comment. I began to listen for different adjectives from "wonderful", "radiant", "sparkling" and "gorgeous". "Delicious" and "divine" also appeared quite often. A few "sensationals". It began to feel rather like a very good review, only instead of reading it, one was hearing it. I think I liked, most of all, the rather softly spoken "ravishingly tempting" from the Lord Chief Justice. I kept wondering if he meant it, particularly when he asked me to dance, just around midnight when the truly memorable moment of our evening occurred.

Lights cross-fade from Victoria to Dexie

Dexie It was as if my body had been took over by an alien force. I started walking towards that bandstand, the microphone like a magnet pulling me to it. It was the means whereby I could tell everyone about their host — the real Sir Marcus Pennington — not the public image Sir Marcus, knighted two years before, heading for greater glory — but the real Marcus with another family in twenty-six Trafalgar Street, Ealing.

Pause

Let's see if I couldn't change some of those smiles to frowns and shock. Where was he anyhow? I couldn't see him in the mob. All penguins look alike. The music just finished as I reached the platform. My heart was thumping louder than the music anyway. I needed a pee

Act II

badly. People were turning back to their tables and suddenly the mike was in my hands. I cleared my throat and the sound echoed across the whole lawn.

Pause

"Ladies and Gentlemen, my name is Dexie Darwin and I come here tonight to say something to Mr Marcus Pennington, that owns this... Sir Marcus Pennington — what owns this whole place and if it wasn't for him you wouldn't be here. My son... I have a son and he wasn't invited here tonight and I wasn't invited here either and we should have been cos—"

Pause

I paused for a second. Everyone had stopped walking back to their seats or talking, all of them now watching me and suddenly there he was, Marcus, pushing his way through to the front of the crowd and I could see the anger in his face as he rushed to the front of these friends of his.

Pause

Our eyes just seemed to lock on each other and then he done the strangest thing. Instead of rushing on to the platform, as I expected, he just stopped dead, shrugged his shoulders and smiled. An actual smile, as if to say, "OK Dexie, you've won. Go ahead, tell the world of our wonderful boy Clifford, my illegitimate son. You've won. I'm sorry." And he just stood there smiling. Suddenly I remembered so clear the first time I seen that magic smile, in my flat, above the Quickspin Laundrette in Ridley Street and I was telling him my broken arm wasn't broke any more. And now suddenly I knew what was broke was my heart.

Pause

In that fraction of a pause, some of the people went to turn away so I started to speak again, looking at Marcus. "— and we should have been invited because — because — although I'm only one of the cleaners at his place of work, we wanted, me and my son to say Happy Birthday, Sir Marcus and thank you for—" I was going to cry, I knew it. I felt the tears starting. "—thank you — for every — for everything."

Pause

Then I turned and fled off that platform, my bladder bursting, straight toward the crowd and like that miracle I heard about in Bible stories long ago, the crowd of people parted before me like the Red Sea as I rushed through them, up towards the house and the Mazda. I dashed through the pathway that opened up before me and I heard Cecil chugging along behind me.

Pause

As I cleared the last of the crowd and was now on the open lawn before the house I thought is that it? Is that what I come all this way to do? To congratulate him on his birthday? Maybe it was and I hadn't known it when I set off with Cecil. Marcus was no longer mine. That I knew but he was still Markie, the father of my son and I couldn't humiliate him on such an occasion. So that was it. But... he had got off lightly! "Make it memorable, Dexie," a little voice said in my head. I turned round. All the crowd was still watching. Cecil was panting by my side. Like a flash I knew what I had to do. I told Cecil what he had to do and he did it.

Lights cross-fade from Dexie to Millicent

Millicent I could not believe my eyes. All my planning and suddenly this... this... this dreadful woman. Appalling!

Lights cross-fade from Millicent to Victoria

Victoria There she was, this cleaning lady, after her simple but so moving little tribute to Marcus, running up the front lawn with her little husband trotting after her, holding his glasses on, when she suddenly stopped, turned to face us all, crouched down and — urinated in front of us all! Meanwhile her little husband stood to attention and saluted beside her and Mitch Mills, joining in the fun, started to play on his trumpet, "Rule Britannia." Absolutely hilarious! Such theatre! Wonderful!

Light stays on Victoria but Millicent's Light also comes on

Millicent Quite disgusting! This cleaner, obviously drunk, with the skimpiest dress one has ever seen, actually squatted on the south lawn and relieved herself not fifty yards from the nearest guests. To my

Act II 51

amazement some of them started to laugh, then cheer and as "Rule Britannia" rang out over the whole proceedings, the entire audience of guests began to cheer and sing. The last night of the proms will never be the same for me again.

The third Light comes up on Dexie. All three Lights are now on

Dexie I had to do it. A birthday party that my Markie would never forget! So down come my pants and I spent not a penny but more like a whole fifty pence worth. It felt so good — all that drink from *The Lady*, all the emotion I had been feeling, all my times with Markie, just seemed to pour out of me. As I listened to that crowd cheering and the trumpeter playing and Cecil chortling beside me, standing and saluting like a frozen statue, I jumped up and at the top of my voice I shouted "Up the Apaches!"

Pause

Two miles from Chessley Park I made Cecil pull over into a lay-by and there in the back of Uncle Fred's Mazda we made love. I knew then that the past was in the past and, despite the dozen red carnations that arrived, without a message, next day, I also knew that Markie was gone.

All Lights lower slightly

And now...
Millicent ...Marcus...
Victoria ...is gone.

Silence for a moment then, swelling in, comes the music of Tony Christie *singing* Is This the Way to Amarilo?

There is the only one light on during the following

Marcus sashays on to the music, mouthing the words, arms up in the air. He moves to Dexie

Dexie laughs

At the chorus break "Boom boom", they knock their hips together in time. After one verse and chorus this music segues into the Irish Ballad Rare Oul Times *sung by* Luke Kelly. *Slowly Dexie and Marcus dance for a time, very close together*

Gradually Marcus breaks away into the darkness and Dexie speaks

Dexie It was fun, Markie, it was fun. We were so young. Even if I could only have you half the time, I had more than many women had, Angie always told me. You were my part-time husband — but my full- time man.

Pause

You know we were lonely at times, Cliff and me, specially when you couldn't be with us at Christmas or some of our birthdays, and that was sad, but — you gave us so much — more than I could ever have give Cliff on his own. What a life he will have — and he loved you so much, as I did.

Pause

It was fun, Markie! Thank you! I don't know what we'll do without you but Apaches are tough. We'll manage and Cecil is so good to us both. Take care wherever you are! Take care, my sweetheart! *Sláinte*!

Lights cross-fade to Millicent

As Marcus walks over to Millicent, she takes off her black coat and is wearing a red dress

Fade in Chris de Burgh *singing* Lady in Red

They dance closely for a time, before he eventually moves away from her into darkness

Millicent I couldn't bring myself to go to the funeral, Marcus. It was for Victoria, the family and all those important folk you knew in high places — not for me.

Pause

At exactly eleven o'clock, I took Cecil for his walk, one that all three of us enjoyed so much. Past the green barn, through the little copse to the stream, over the old log bridge, left along the bank to the Fennies, then across the field to the road and back home.

Act II 53

Pause

I felt you were with us, my dearest, all the way, so I'm afraid I chatted to you most of the time. That confused poor old Cecil dreadfully. He kept looking round for you so I told him all about us, of our happy times together and why you couldn't be with us as much as you wanted. Silly, I know, but I believe he understood.

Pause

When we got home, the funeral would have been all over. So we had each said goodbye in our own, separate ways. They sang hymns and prayed for your soul. We walked by the green barn and the pebble stream and I told you again that you had my heart for ever.

Pause

Then I opened some soup and sat listening to the most romantic music you ever gave me, Sibelius and *Finlandia*, of course, to speed you on your way. I'm not sure where that will be but I know that, if possible, Clifford will be waiting there to greet you. What a joy that will be for you both. My two favourite men! Goodbye, my dearest one.

Lights cross-fade to Victoria

Marcus walks to Victoria as the music fades in of Ella Fitzgerald singing the chorus of Someone to Watch Over Me

They dance closely together. As the song ends, Marcus leaves into darkness

Victoria Goodbye, my darling! You always said that, before me, you would exit (*smiling*) pursued by a bare — female of some kind, preferably from the Swedish sauna.

Pause

It was an impressive finale, my darling. You certainly packed them in. House full! All Hallows has never had standing room only before. Three from the Lords, Sir Dudley and Sir Geoffrey from the High Court and that frightful Amazon in tweeds, yet again, from the Foreign Office, or is it the Home Office? And so many of my own colleagues from the theatre. Max from the National, Terry and Alison from the

Beeb, Roger Regus and poor Barry, almost unable to walk now, even to my amazement, Rona and her new Polish husband number four. Not even half her age and with no English at all. Rona was quite tearful, seemed very upset – just like her Desdemona. Very OTT.

Pause

Claudia, Beatrice and I — we all love you; Arthur, Julius and the children. Goodbye my darling — until the next act! "May flights of angels sing thee to thy rest." Goodbye.

Someone to Watch Over Me *fades in and plays quietly*

All three Lights come up slightly on the three women in tableau and then fade to Black-out

THE END

FURNITURE AND PROPERTY LIST

ACT I

On stage: Chairs
Screens
Lamps
Small tables
Ornaments
Coat stand

ACT II

On stage: A glass
A bottle of whisky

Personal: **Victoria**: letters, a bag. *In it:* photographs

LIGHTING PLOT

Practical fitting required: nil
1 interior. The same scene throughout

ACT I

To open: Light on Victoria

| Cue 1 | **Victoria**: "We are all soap operas really." *Lights cross-fade to Millicent* | (Page 2) |

| Cue 2 | **Millicent**: "...but interesting, one must admit." *Lights cross-fade to Dexie* | (Page 3) |

| Cue 3 | **Dexie**: "...when they're interested. Know what I mean *Lights cross-fade to Victoria* | (Page 4) |

| Cue 4 | **Victoria**: "Why, Claudia of course." *Lights cross-fade to Millicent* | (Page 7) |

| Cue 5 | **Millicent**: "He said, "we'll go out." " *Lights cross-fade to Dexie* | (Page 9) |

| Cue 6 | **Dexie**: "...but I reckoned I had his number." *Lights cross-fade to Victoria* | (Page 10) |

| Cue 7 | **Victoria**: "...something like "Not so bloody loud." " *Lights cross-fade to Millicent* | (Page 11) |

| Cue 8 | **Millicent**: "...for a run up to the cemetery, this evening *Lights cross-fade to Dexie* | (Page 13) |

| Cue 9 | **Dexie**: "He didn't call the next week, nor the next." *Lights cross-fade to Victoria* | (Page 15) |

| Cue 10 | **Victoria**: "...soothing platitudes. How ghastly!" *Lights cross-fade to Dexie* | (Page 16) |

| Cue 11 | **Dexie**: "No rest for the wicked." *Lights cross-fade to Millicent* | (Page 17) |

Lighting Plot

Cue 12	**Millicent**: "And I did, on so many occasions." *Lights cross-fade from Millicent to general dim lighting*	(Page 19)
Cue 13	**Victoria**: "'Night, darling!" and exits **Marcus** watches her and smiles *Lights fade to Black-out*	(Page 21)

ACT II

To open: Light on Victoria

Cue 14	**Victoria**: "...instead of being at a conference in Edinburgh." *Lights cross-fade to Dexie*	(Page 23)
Cue 15	**Dexie**: "You want your son to be born a Scotsman?" *Lights cross-fade to Victoria*	(Page 24)
Cue 16	**Victoria**: "His mind would be on matters other than family." *Lights cross-fade to Dexie*	(Page 25)
Cue 17	**Dexie**: "...he was such a good barrister — so bloody quick." *Lights cross-fade to Millicent*	(Page 26)
Cue 18	**Millicent**: "...must slip down so easily, Mills." And it did. *Lights cross-fade to Dexie*	(Page 27)
Cue 19	**Dexie**: "...never appeared in out little son's vocabulary." *Lights cross-fade to Victoria*	(Page 29)
Cue 20	**Victoria**: " "...of outrageous fortune" and all that!" *Lights cross-fade to Millicent*	(Page 31)
Cue 21	**Millicent**: "Now, could you imagine Clifford behaving like that?" *Lights cross-fade to Dexie*	(Page 31)
Cue 22	**Dexie**: "...the craic is not going to be mighty!" *Lights cross-fade to Victoria*	(Page 33)
Cue 23	**Victoria**: "No one could ever make me laugh like Marcus." *Lights cross-fade to Millicent*	(Page 35)

Cue 24	**Millicent**: "He just didn't always realize that." *Lights cross-fade to Dexie*	(Page 36)
Cue 25	**Dexie**: "But I knew then I had lost Marcus for good." *Lights cross-fade to Victoria*	(Page 38)
Cue 26	**Victoria**: "Now why was I telling you about that? Oh, yes." *Lights cross-fade to Millicent*	(Page 38)
Cue 27	**Millicent**: "...Victoria planning anything. I should ring her." *Lights cross-fade to Victoria*	(Page 39)
Cue 28	**Victoria**: "...and we all we went to see the very moving Someone Who'll Watch Over Me." *Lights cross-fade to Millicent*	(Page 40)
Cue 29	**Millicent**: "Oh what a tangled web we weave..." *Lights cross-fade to Victoria*	(Page 42)
Cue 30	**Victoria**: "How would you like to arrange a party?" *Lights cross-fade to Millicent*	(Page 42)
Cue 31	**Millicent**: "*The Ritz*, the *Savoy* or the *Connaught*?' " *Lights cross-fade to Dexie*	(Page 43)
Cue 30	**Dexie**: "The question was what to do about it." *Lights cross-fade to Millicent*	(Page 43)
Cue 31	**Millicent**: "Personae very non gratae!" *Lights cross-fade to Victoria*	(Page 43)
Cue 32	**Victoria**: "...dogs in every drawer. Sandy wouldn't have it." *Lights cross-fade to Dexie*	(Page 44)
Cue 33	**Dexie**: "Who would want a toeless ten-year-old?" *Lights cross-fade to Victoria*	(Page 44)
Cue 34	**Victoria**: "...was a risk I was not prepared to take." *Lights cross-fade to Millicent*	(Page 44)
Cue 35	**Millicent**: "It would be a wonderful occasion." *Light cross-fade to Dexie*	(Page 45)

Lighting Plot

Cue 36	**Millicent**: " "Not exactly," I said." *Lights cross-fade to Victoria*	(Page 45)
Cue 37	**Victoria**: "...the temperature of the pate on such an evening?" *Lights cross-fade to Millicent*	(Page 45)
Cue 38	**Millicent**: "...I've resurrected the *Mexican Midnight*." *Lights cross-fade to Dexie*	(Page 46)
Cue 39	**Dexie**: " "We're going for a drive in the *Mazda*." " *Lights cross-fade to Victoria*	(Page 46)
Cue 40	**Victoria**: "...and what a dress! *Gucci* or *Givenchy*?" *Lights cross-fade to Dexie*	(Page 46)
Cue 41	**Dexie**: "...and touched his forehead." *Lights cross-fade to Millicent*	(Page 47)
Cue 42	**Millicent**: "...she'd ever heard a *Sibelius* Symphony?" *Lights cross-fade to Victoria*	(Page 48)
Cue 43	**Victoria**: "...memorable moment of our evening occurred." *Lights cross-fade to Dexie*	(Page 48)
Cue 44	**Dexie**: "I told Cecil what he had to do and he did it." *Lights cross-fade to Millicent*	(Page 50)
Cue 45	**Millicent**: "... this dreadful woman. Appalling!" *Lights cross-fade to Victoria*	(Page 50)
Cue 46	**Victoria**: "Such theatre! Wonderful!" *Light comes up on Millicent*	(Page 50)
Cue 47	**Millicent**: "...will never be the same for me again." *Light comes up on Dexie*	(Page 51)
Cue 48	**Dexie**: "I also knew that Markie was gone." *All Lights lower slightly*	(Page 51)
Cue 49	**Dexie** and **Marcus** dance for a time, very close together *Only Light on their scene together*	(Page 51)
Cue 50	**Dexie**: "Take care, my sweetheart! *Sláinte*!" *Lights cross-fade to Millicent*	(Page 52)

Cue 51	**Millicent**: "My two favourite men! Goodbye, my dearest one." *Lights cross-fade to Victoria*	(Page 53)
Cue 52	"Someone to Watch Over me" fades in *Three Lights come up slightly on three women and then fade to Black-out*	(Page 54)

EFFECTS PLOT

ACT I

No cues

ACT II

Cue 1	**Victoria**: "is gone." *Music: Is This the Way to Amarilo?*	(Page 51)
Cue 2	**Marcus** and **Dexie** knock their hips together *Music : Irish Ballad "Rare Oul Times"*	(Page 51)
Cue 3	**Marcus** walks over to **Millicent**. She takes off her coat *Music "Lady in Red"*	(Page 52)
Cue 4	Lights cross-fade to **Victoria** and **Marcus** walks to her *Music "Someone to Watch Over Me" fades in*	(Page 53)
Cue 5	**Victoria**: " "...sing thee to thy rest." Goodbye." *Music "Someone to Watch Over Me" fades in*	(Page 54)

Use of Copyright Music

A licence issued by Samuel French Ltd to perform this play does not include permission to use any Incidental music specified in this copy. Where the place of performance is already licensed by the PERFORMING RIGHT SOCIETY a return of the music used must be made to them. If the place of performance is not so licensed then application should be made to the Performing Right Society, 29 Berners Street, London Wl.

A separate and additional licence from PHONOGRAPHIC PERFORMANCES LTD, 1 Upper James Street, London W1R 3HG is needed whenever commercial recordings are used.

www.ingramcontent.com/pod-product-compliance
Ingram Content Group UK Ltd.
Pitfield, Milton Keynes, MK11 3LW, UK
UKHW021842140426
5217IPUK00022B/1552